Bad Dog, Andy

A Parody by Cassandra Peterson and John Paragon

Illustrated by Cathy Pavia

Publisher: W. Quay Hays
Editorial Director: Peter L. Hoffman
Production Director: Trudihope Schlomowitz
Prepress Manager: Bill Castillo
Production Artist: Gaston Moraga
Production Assistant: Russel Lockwood

Copyright © 1997 by Cassandra Peterson and John Paragon

For Sadie

All rights reserved under International and Pan-American Copyright Conventions. This book, or any parts thereof, may not be reproduced in any fashion whatsoever without the prior written permission of the Publisher.

For information:

General Publishing Group, Inc.
2701 Ocean Park Boulevard, Suite 140
Santa Monica, CA 90405

DISCLAIMER

Bad Dog, Andy is a parody of Alexandra Day's best-seller, *Good Dog, Carl*. True to the spirit of parody, we disclaim any approval or endorsement from Ms. Day and her publisher and trust that no one would confuse our respective works.

Library of Congress Cataloging-in-Publication Data

Peterson, Cassandra
    Bad dog, Andy / by Cassandra Peterson and John Paragon ;
illustrated by Cathy Pavia.
        p. cm.
    ISBN 1-57544-037-7
    1. Dogs—Humor   I. Paragon, John. II. Pavia, Cathy. III. Title.
PN6231.P3E58 1997
741.5'973—dc21   97-40431
                                                                                CIP

Printed in Mexico
10 9 8 7 6 5 4 3 2 1
General Publishing Group, Inc.
Los Angeles

"Andy, stay here and watch the house. I'll be back soon."

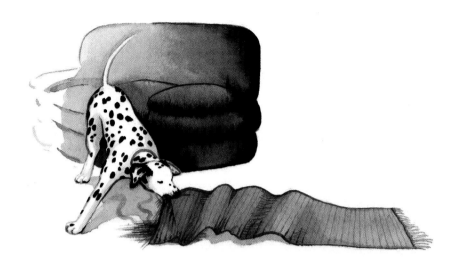

"Bad dog, Andy!"

Photo by Michael Maron

Cassandra Peterson is better known as her infamous character Elvira, Mistress of the Dark. Her acting and writing credits include her syndicated series, "Movie Macabre," her own feature film, *Elvira, Mistress of the Dark*, and her recently released series of horror/comedy novels (Berkley Publishing) titled *Elvira's Nightmares*, cowritten by her longtime writing partner, John Paragon. She is the proud owner of a very well-behaved Rottweiler, Bram.

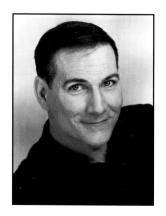

John Paragon is an actor/writer/director who has cowritten numerous Elvira projects with Ms. Peterson since Elvira's inception. In addition, he performed in and was a writer/director of the popular ABC television show, "Pee-Wee's Playhouse." He has recently appeared on the hit comedy show "Seinfeld" and directed episodic television, including "Silk Stalkings" and "Pacific Blue" for the USA Network. He is the long-suffering owner of an adorable, but sometimes naughty Dalmatian named, uh, Andy.

Photo by Alan Shaffer

Cathy Pavia is a graduate of the Cleveland Institute of Art. Her illustrations are featured in a variety of magazines, books, and advertising campaigns. Serving as an art lecturer and instructor for several Southern California universities, her work is also showcased in many galleries and selected exhibitions. Cathy shares her home with a husband and two coonhounds who, incidentally, are all very bad.